AF324000

A Single Flower

Meditations & Poems

heart wisdom
— press —

A
Single
Flower

PHILIP M. BERK

NATIONAL
LIBRARY
OF AUSTRALIA

*For the possibility of peace within ourselves and within our world.
May this peace spread in the four directions across our precious Mother Earth.*

Praise for Philip M. Berk

"While living in challenging and uncertain times, Berk's poetry inspires us on how to keep our light shining. I will definitely keep it close to me to read when I need to remember the truth of who I am and how to surrender to the perfection of the universe....it is brillliant"

—Sandra Ingerman,
author of *Medicine for the Earth*

"Reading Philip M. Berk's wonderful and healing book is like breaking fresh baked bread to nourish our hungry soul."

—Hank Wesselman, Ph.D.,
author of *Spirit Medicine*

"An ecstatic expression that will bring joy and inspiration to anyone who reads it. This book is a precious gift."

—Larry Dossey, MD,
author of *One Mind*

"Berk's poetry is a treasure to be used for your spiritual growth and practice. Each gem starts you on a flight of consciousness to the realm where your soul lives."

—Rabbi Zalman Schachter-Shalomi,
author of *From Age-Ing to Sage-Ing*

"....an elixir of truth"

—Marianne Williamson,
author of *A Return to Love*

CONTENTS

If we could see the miracle
of a single flower clearly,
our whole life would change.

Gautama Buddha

⌘

TEACHINGS ON A SINGLE FLOWER

∽

A LIFETIME

CB

We all are faced with the fleetingness of time. We are going to live only a short while. A lifetime is not very long. We have to make the decision: are we going to live this short amount of time with fear and resistance, not living the life we could have, not being the person we could have, or are we going to step forward and greet this unique chance of a lifetime with openness, acceptance, and love?

AS IT IS

ଔ

When there is love, there is no more resistance to what is. Love brings you into the moment with open arms, open to whatever is. Knowing that it is, as it is - *perfect*.

EMBRACE YOURSELF

 CŞ

Now is a palace where you sit unmoved by the turmoil in your life and the futilities in your mind. Now is a dance that requires you to stand up, embrace yourself, and cast the rusty old shackles away.

THE PRESENT MOMENT

രു

Relaxing in the presence of stillness, accepting with the feeling of gratitude, opening up to the wisdom that you are fully taken care of — this is what happens when you enter the present moment.

THE CHOICE

The quality of your life depends on how you respond to whatever life presents you. You can greet life's uncertainties with patience and trust or you can greet them with resistance and fear. The choice is completely yours.

AS YOU ARE

☙

There is no better medicine than loving yourself. There is no better cure than allowing yourself to be as you are. It is time to let your truth burn inside of you like a million suns lighting up your way; like a galaxy of love surrounding your every breath.

TRUE PRACTICE

❦

Further yourself and face all that frightens you. Turn your obstacles into allies. Strengthen your capacity to connect to all things. Connecting and persevering—this is the foundation of true practice.

RIVER'S WISDOM

C３

Let the river's wisdom drench you. Let the continual stream of change rush through you. Be as fluid and graceful as a dancer moving with the current. Lose yourself and life will unfold with ease. You will feel the presence of peace within everything that you do.

PURE BEING

❧

Let go of fear and realize love. Let go of hurt and realize peace. Let go of yourself and realize bliss. Why not experience this absolute bliss and ecstasy of pure being? Why not experience the absolute paradise and heaven of living in love?

WHEN YOU RETURN

ℭℜ

When you return to joy, you return to yourself. When you return to love, you return to the source. When you return to your soul, you return home.

ALL THE POWER IN THE COSMOS

Energy is the flow of space and time merging with the wild and raw nature of existence. Feel this flow and know that you can harness and ride it. You can breathe it in each and every moment. All the power in the cosmos is nowhere but within you.

PEACE

Be still and quiet within — find your true presence. Live within this presence — do not worry about expectations; do not concern yourself with outcomes. Firm in yourself and in your own conviction, you will always be at peace.

LETTING GO

ℭ

Letting go is the continual teaching. Let go. Let go. Let go. And fall; into grace, into wisdom, into love—receive: a peaceful mind, a compassionate heart, an awakened soul.

SOUL PURPOSE

଎

When you purify fear's constant projections, you will see your clear intention of birth—your soul purpose—your reason for walking this Earth.

SIMPLY BE

ೞ

Feel the entire universe residing in your being. Know there is nothing to ever search for outside of yourself. Experience the world in perfect harmony. Experience yourself as part of this harmony. Feel divinity in yourself and in all of creation. Simply be, and witness this miraculous unfolding.

FEARLESS

ೞ

When you trust, you allow yourself to let go.
When you let go, you free yourself from doubt.
When you are free from doubt, you become *fearless*.

INFINITE POSSIBILITY

ↂ

In this very moment you hold the key to overcoming every obstacle, unfolding every blessing, and discovering the infinite possibility of love and life. This very moment is the revelation of all of creation.

TRANSFORM THIS PLACE RIGHT NOW

ର

Listen to this love that speaks directly to the heart, it says: "Transform this place right now into the space of radiant possibility!"

SELF-TRANSFORMATION

ের

We are always moving in and out of change. We are always in a constant state of becoming. We never arrive at a place where we do not have to face the challenge of self-transformation. Self-transformation is our continual task.

THE LOTUS

ॐ

Life is always testing your limits and the more you engage in this process, the more you inevitably feel pain—but it is what you do with the pain that matters. Just as the lotus grows out of the mud, you grow through the tests and trials that your heart endures. Your experiences, no matter how hard, are the tools for you to use to embrace your life.

OPEN

Cℛ

With your body open and relaxed, experience the truth of this new moment. With your mind open and awake, perceive the true nature of reality. With your heart open and pure, receive the many blessings of life. With your soul open and connected, awaken and inspire your great presence.

THE GROUND OF BEING

ॐ

The ground in which you reside is eternal, never changing, throughout all the ages, throughout all our stages. Yet we rise and fall, again and again, like a flower blooming and wilting, always regenerating, always transforming. We are always spiraling inwards to reach the soul. Through the majesty of love, the ground of everlasting being, we are made whole.

AWAKENING

Fear causes you to doubt who you are. Fear causes you to lose sight of your soul purpose in life, which is to love and live freely within this unique expression of love. Fear can be eliminated through the full acceptance and complete trust in the life process. Through acceptance and trust you let go of your need for control. As you begin to let go, you clear yourself of all unnecessary burdens that do not serve your highest good. Being free from fear, life becomes a miraculous unfolding into self-realization and self-awakening.

MIRACLES

ॐ

Love mends all. Only love can make whatever is broken whole again. With love as your deepest prayer, miracles unfold.

ABUNDANCE

Abundance isn't something you have to create. It is already inside you and all around you. You simply need to open your heart to receive it.

HEALING

❦

Allow yourself to be embraced by the power of love and the process of healing naturally unfolds. Allow yourself to be healed and the process of life naturally flourishes.

YOUR SOUL

CX

Your soul is your own unique expression of Spirit that is eternal, interconnected to all things, perfect, and whole. When you connect to this presence, you unfold a wisdom that transcends the physical limitations of this world. Your soul is your spiritual vehicle that transports you through time and space, through the Great Mystery of creation.

FEAR OR LOVE?

⌒

Your thoughts either come from fear or they come from love. Fear based thoughts root from a feeling of needing to control the external world. Fear creates a feeling of separateness between yourself and your environment. Fear promotes the feeling: "What about me?" This ongoing struggle creates disharmony, aggression, and chaos. Love based thoughts, on the other hand, allow you to feel your interconnectedness to all that is. Feeling one with all that is, you are able to let go and experience your true nature—which is boundless freedom and bliss.

THE REALIZATION OF SPIRIT

❧

When you awaken to the realization that nothing is separate from Spirit, you see divinity within yourself and within all of life. This realization of Spirit allows you to transcend every limitation imaginable. Spirit does not know limitations. Spirit has limitless potential, and because Spirit is what you are, you too have limitless potential.

COMPASSION

 C ompassion is the medicine for the affliction of suffering. It heals your heart with gentleness. It heals your heart with loving kindness. It allows life to be redeemed and for love to be revealed.

THE SOURCE

∞

When you access the source and follow its course, you flow like a river always at ease. You stand like a mountain always at peace. You welcome every experience as it comes, always giving yourself away like the Sun with its rays—lighting, embracing, and welcoming each new day.

A SINGLE FLOWER

Awaken your inner presence of divinity—allow it to flower as a lotus from within. This blossoming of love and joy is your birthright.

CONTENTMENT

໨

It only takes one moment to peel the thick layers of self that hide the core of your being and feel the warmth of the eternal Sun. This warmth flows from the healing light of your soul. When you are enveloped in this light, you know that you no longer need anything—that you have everything—because you realize you are everything. It is this very feeling, this innate wisdom that arises from your soul, which gives birth to inner peace and contentment.

ALCHEMY

ℭ℞

Become a magician of thought and disappear fear. Work skillfully with the art of illusion, understanding the cosmic fusion of the elements. Then, like an alchemist, transform your doubt and hesitation into the heart opening of appreciation.

LOVE AS YOUR COMPASS

ॐ

Break open the luminous light inside your innermost being. Give yourself away freely to this mystery of love which heals. Reach out fearlessly. Feel everything courageously. Allow yourself to always learn and grow. With love as your compass, free fall into the unknown.

THE JOURNEY

Healing is the journey.
The destination is yourself.

ENLIGHTEN

❧

Through the ordinary discover the extraordinary.

By seeing the unseen, enlighten all your days.

THE PATH AND THE GOAL

☙

By letting things come and go, you accord with the natural flow of things. You see how you are in all things and all things are in you. Inwardly know that there is nothing to achieve—that you are the path and the goal.

SACRED SPACE

ℭℜ

Pierce the dark shadows with the energy of love.

Enter sacred space that is your heart's rightful home.

GRATEFUL HEART

ભ

You are forever moving through realms of dream illusion. Your task is to capture moments with love and then deliver them back unto creation. Weave your grateful heart into the eternal dream, expressing what longs to be free, in this moment of cosmic proportions.

THERE IS NO END

ॐ

There is no end to where you begin. So let go and bend the rules. Rearrange your thoughts. Redefine reality from the sorrow of time to the endless creative fervor of the Divine.

INSPIRE HOLINESS

ʘ

Your work is to multiply compassion with kindness and create uplifted equations of worthiness. Your daily work is to shake off conditioning and inspire holiness.

ALL IS POSSIBLE

ᘍ

Open your cells to receive. Open your thoughts to believe. All is possible within this universe of form. All is possible. As energy is neither created nor destroyed, only continually and lovingly transformed.

REARRANGE YOUR FATE

೧

Move with the planets of change. Celebrate life and rearrange your fate. Do not be afraid—to touch inner space and transform outer place.

UNIFY YOURSELF

☙

No longer caught up in distinctions that limit the mystery of creation, open yourself with spontaneity, forget yourself with humility, bow down respectfully. Greet each new experience as it comes, unify yourself and the moment into one.

SACRED GEOMETRY

ᴄᴢ

Through life's all pervasive relationships and fractals of transformation and information, through this creative abundance of ever malleable energy, this sacred geometry—touch what breathes beneath this holographic surface. Listen carefully and hear, the music of the spheres.

MOVE MIRACLES

 love is the invisible realm where you gather light to move miracles. As a lover of life defy that which is seen. Move freely inside of dreams.

OPEN SKY

ભ

This thirst for life burns for experience, openness, presence—the willingness to be open sky—to harness light, to fly.

MOST IMPORTANT

ॐ

Possess what is most important, which is not the body and the things of this world, but the beauty of the Spirit and the truth of the eternal.

DREAM OF LIFE

ᙣ

Rest your weary head. Look around, all has turned to dust. The dream of life continues and the tremors of night still are calling. You can no longer break away from that which opens you.

TRUTH

Fill the air with truth.

Give yourself to what you cannot claim.

EVER GIVING LIGHT

Remember the truth of the soul that this world can help you so easily forget. The truth is that love is the holy source of your life. Love is where you start and where you return. Love is the beginning and the end. Love is the source of all creation, the ever giving light that transcends.

DISTANCE OF LOVE

ை

You are a soul traveller, a mystic dancer, crossing the distance of love from one perimeter of space to another.

POETRY TO INSPIRE THE SOUL

COME WITH ME

Tonight
I will be your starry magician

I will open to you
the great hollow skies of the unknown

From pure nothingness,
I will transform your weary eyes of form

Reveal to you a brilliant light—

Transformed
through infinite time, space, and darkness

I will enlighten
these moments of emptiness

Come with me,
my love

⌘

THE MIRACULOUS

Grab hold
of the miraculous
and attune yourself
to the infinite

Because everything
is vibration,
harmonize yourself
to cosmic frequencies

Because everything
is love,
resonate with
all of creation

Deep inside
hear
a silent, unfathomable
echo

Deep inside
feel
a mystical, enlightening
breath

⌘

THIS HEART THAT BEATS

This mystic love
calls to your every moment
as witness as breath

But can you reach inside
and melt this ego
made of illusion
and death?

Can you mold
your sorrow
and transform your fear
into devotion
and presence?

For you are standing
in the middle of the field
of divine providence

Yes you are alone—
but you are not kept separate
from divinity

This heart that beats
is for all to see

⌘

SPIRAL OPEN

Move stars
from within

and birth light

Soar into the galaxy
where lovers meet
and caress
eternity

Spiral open—

Transform distances of fear
as your birthright
of dreams

Remember: you are a dreamer
of mind
and as you create,
so you are

⌘

BURNING EMBERS

Who are we to fight
this uproar of burning embers?
We who long to learn
but cannot bear to be burned

Catapult us into our spinning orbits

For time is so short
Born and die in one blink of an eye

We have come to be known
not to waste away in oblivion and
never grow

Look how the tides turn
Look how evening glows
Look how each day is a longing
to behold

Step into these embers
where the Sun
beckons you by name

Where lovers stare into the light
not scared of the flame

⌘

ARCHITECT

Our lives are a mere dream—so take heed
and free what exists
within your soul's depths

Free yourself from the bondage of death
by turning the dial
of your perception

Know that this world
is but a kaleidoscope image
of conception

So astral project
beyond all
limitation

Soar inside of dreams
to inspire
creative imagination

Know that you are the architect
of your own
happiness

Imbue your spirit
with the endless possibility
of eternal emptiness

⌘

BORN IN STARS

Ancient secrets
that are born in stars
dance
in the dream light

Where sadness
is born again,
where fear
grows wings

Where you transform
sorrow and suffering
into a song
that illumines all things

⌘

DREAM CATCHER

Free
inside of dreams
where there is no gravity
to hold you down

No reality to keep you bound

Because you are as boundless
as eternal light,
lost and yet found

Orbiting the perimeters of years

Shooting stars of moments
that pass by inside of fears

You are the dream catcher
inside this universe of loss

You are the freedom rider
moving right through and across—

this world of tears

⌘

DREAM WEAVER

My love, there are shadows in your eyes
These dark places where you can no longer see

For you have grown cold in the wilderness
of perception

This great magic trick of the senses has left you whirlwinded

By these shadow men who wield ignorance
and deception

But the dream weaver weaves an endless dream
of spiritual truth and realization

And right now you are taking part
in wielding your very own thoughts
into creation

You who live inside of infinite and overlapping
dimensions of divine illumination

Your only chance at freeing your heart
is to shine this light
unto all death and destruction

To turn your suffering into bliss

To make your way
where all seems dark and scary

And to be a willing witness

In this great and redeeming play
of consciousness

⌘

CIRCLE OF IMPERMANENCE

Inside of emptiness
you feel bare,
vulnerable,
naked,
yet full

Like that circle
of impermanence
that tears

Open
life and love
to dance
in the spheres
of change,
these lines
of time
that cage you,
yet break you

Open
endlessly
into flow—
so you can sow
your seeds,
allow yourself
to be free—
ephemeral—

NOW

⌘

SILENT CORRIDOR OF STARS

If you listen
you will hear
the glorious melody
that echoes inside

Far from the noisy
highways of self

You will hear
the silent corridor
of stars
moving inwards

This light—

this light
is the holy
breath
of

God

⌘

YOU ARE THE SEED

In this world's endless shadows
of deception

In the ego's dark corners
of fear and rejection

Persist in remembering that you are the seed
of all creation

Your inner nature is that of light—
which is a profound revelation

Oh friend with heavy heart,
break open these vast reservoirs of truth inside

This inner wisdom that shines
as a radiant jewel of the Divine

And forget these shadows of ignorance
that only cast doubt
about who you truly are

Which is not this chaos mess delirium
of vanity, greed, violence, and materialism

No, for you are born of holiness and stars!

You were born to witness the miraculous unfolding
of love and light inside your very own heart!

⌘

BLESSING OF LIFE

Corruption
cannot hide
the miraculous light
of the Divine

For the power of Spirit
is beyond all control

And the soul
is eternal and free

Lend me your ear, friend

No one can bind you to misery
or to fear

You have within you shards of invisible wings

Draw your open heart near
and begin to understand

Know that the Earth beneath you
is holy ground

And the air you breathe
is holy air

And this blessing of life
that you receive

Can never be diminished by man

⌘

PRAISE

Move the great flood
of reckoning
from within

Mystery to mystery,
begin

Like water,
touch the deep depths
of Earth

For the reasons of life,
give yourself to darkness
and birth

Water the seed
of your belief
through praising

Praise this endless river
of dreams,
this holy river of light!

⌘

MEET ME HERE

Meet me in the tunnel
of twilight

Between the shadows
and the light

Here in the echo
of endless silence

Deep in the ruins—

Meet me here

Inside the caverns
of your empty heart

Inside,
and never apart

⌘

THE INNER SEA
AND VAST SPACIOUSNESS OF BEING

This empty space of tears
and longing

This light that fills the heart
with memory and meaning

This opening within creation
that allows the breath to flow

This is the place
where the heart beats holy

This is where the mind wakes
from the illusion of reality

This is the majesty
of love

This is the brilliance
of soul

This is the deliverance
of all things

This is the suffering
and the healing

This is the inner sea
and vast spaciousness of being

⌘

ASCENSION

Your tears formed
a white river
of possibility

So you jumped
recklessly
in

Singing of your soul
and morning's
fervent song

(Love finally found a way in)

You ascended
from the depths of sorrow

Lifted yourself up

Into a new life

Ready
for
anything

⌘

YOUR POTENTIAL FOR DIVINITY

Feel the Sun
of synchronicity
shining
on your potential
for divinity

In this garden
of days,
where you are
what you think

Where you can change
belief
in one blink of the eye

And expand your view of
yourself
and all your I's

So let go
of all
limited perception

Look out
your soul-window
and see

Sun blazed, golden, joyous
pure light
of uncarved expression

⌘

IMPERMANENCE

Through the looking glass
as each day passes

Behold each moment
with tender glances

Liberate the shadows that persist
in the loneliness

This fear of loss
that permeates

The hollowness—

The broken song of innocence

This opening in which
the breadth
of death
creates a myriad
play of consciousness

Through a divine brilliance—

An ephemeral light show
of life, love, and experience

Breathe this in and be a witness

To what is ever fleeting and precious!

⌘

AS ABOVE, SO BELOW

As above
so below
Between suffering
and love
Between light
and shadow
Between ego
and soul
We are always
being opened
In this ever present void
To learn
To grow

⌘

SORROW

What is sorrow
but a seed
of possibility

What is loss
but an expanding universe,
an endless dimension
of probability,
where you are
a simple idea
floating
as a feather
on eternity

⌘

THE FOREVER SIGH OF THE UNIVERSE

Light born through form
that dances
in the forever sigh of the universe
is right before your very eyes

This light
is 13.8 billion years old
and how will you behold
such majesty?

In one blink of an eye
of a lifetime—
this miracle
of love
that bore you

This brilliance of body
and mind—
this mystery
of life
that has blessed you

And how will you
express this moment
of time?

⌘

DIVINE SPARK

Be the mystery
mirage
and revelation
of knowing the truth
in the great
cosmic undertaking
that is you

Allow life
to bloom fully inside
as light
that is birthed
in the holy dark womb
of Mother

And you
the divine spark—
the eternal
Lover

⌘

DARK MYSTERY

Dark mystery
too profound to touch

Yet the soul reaches for water
deep in this abyss

Feel the darkness
in which you are turning

Fall like dust
into the palms of your hidden self

Hold to the invisible realm
in which you float on dreams

Into the arms of the Goddess
made of time and eternity

⌘

WHAT LIVES WITHIN THE HEART

Love came forward
and spoke

About the
broken heart

About
the soul

About time's yearning
and loss

Love says:
'Fear Not'

For what lives
within
the heart

Is
always
kept safe

And is never lost

⌘

LUMINOUS

You are the trace
of soul
and infinity

A fleeting image
of light
and shadow
across the illusory
screen
of reality

You
are but
shards of light
and time
and memory

Dive freely
into this luminous space
of becoming!

Into this completion

This—our universal destiny

⌘

LIMITLESS SUN

This seed of possibility
This, the Sun's divinity

Rays of light that open
you into time
from eternity

For you are eternity's love for time

This limitless Sun of pure being
allows lifetimes to unfold

In the house of mind
Through the window of soul

This blissful Sun shines
Divine
As your eternal home

⌘

TREATISE ON THE TRUTH OF ONENESS

I

We have come to this ancient dwelling of Earth as an undying wish in the empty and glorious well of the heart. We have come for the longing inside is so great that it trembles in the dark eternal void and births the illusion of the other. This "other" is the reflection of our separate self.

II

This relationship of duality illuminates all of time and space. This bright illumination of mind creates our myriad illusion of reality. We dance within these endless fractals of energy. We are ever changing and being born again and again through this heavenly light of creation.

III

We are but a child of life as we move within the parameters of birth and death to experience the great majesty of the heart. Our divine parents, emptiness and consciousness, support our journey through the cosmos.

IV

We travel through infinite planes of consciousness to unravel the many mysteries of the heart.

V

The heart is the source of all wisdom. All wisdom comes from the trials of suffering that the heart endures.

VI

The heart is the pathway to love and love is boundless energy. Love is eternal. Love transcends time and space. Love is the unifying force beyond duality.

VII

Listen carefully to what the heart has
to say, to what information and mem-
ories it carries.

VIII

Search your heart's mysterious land-
scape of dreams and images. Listen to
the deep resonance of spiritual truth
that lies at its very core.

IX

The nature of duality and opposites on this plane of existence often confuses our senses and can block the heart's ability to perceive the spiritual truth of Oneness.

X

Life becomes a struggle when our devotion is to the material things of the external world and not the inherent divinity and totality of the heart.

XI

Always needing to consume—to be secure—to fulfill its own needs, this massive force of mind, called Ego, has a shadow side that is currently destroying our planet Earth.

XII

This destruction persists through the illusion of separateness. Separateness promotes the feeling of fear, and fear is what feeds the dark shadows of the ego mind.

XIII

Ego has the potential to destroy nature
as it consumes everything in its path
looking for its own security, for greed
is the force behind all destructiveness.

XIV

If ego is allowed to rule the mind,
control eventually manifests itself
into dominance, dominance manifests
itself into greed—and greed eventually
poisons the heart and contaminates
the human spirit. Selfishness is the
root of all evil.

XV

It is only through the lens of perception that the ego and our experience of fear exist, so it is through perception that this can be corrected. This is done through a refocusing of one's attention.

XVI

If ego is not corrected, it pollutes the human spirit through ideas of ownership.

XVII

Ideas of ownership create an ignorance
that is the root of all suffering, even
that of death.

XVIII

Ideas of ownership create an ongoing
obsession with the external world of
appearances. This external preoc-
cupation with the world of matter
drives the ego's incessant need to
dominate and rule.

XIX

The only way to overcome this oppressive force of mind is through the awakening of humility in one's heart space.

XX

Humility allows your ego to see itself as an interconnected, interdependent, and interrelated part of a greater whole. This healing vision is that you and everything else in the Universe are One.

XXI

This healing vision allows the ego to rest in its appropriate place. It also allows the ego, the separate self, to surrender its constant need for control.

XXII

The art of surrender creates a space for the ego to unfold the limitless nature of Spirit versus the limited nature of self.

XXIII

The overwhelming, awe inspiring and peaceful presence of Spirit is a radiant elixir that heals and transforms all dark shadows of the ego mind. This divine presence evaporates the dualities of mind.

XXIV

This space of humility is garnered through the diligent practice of letting go of fixed mind and the practice of loving others and nature as yourself.

XXV

It is important to remember that the world is but a shared view of reality that is sustained through feelings and beliefs. The world can change in an instant. The world is the result of the collective thought process that is in constant flux and motion.

XXVI

We always have a choice with how we engage with our minds, so ultimately this world is in our very own hands. Our minds, reality, the world, and our perceptions are inexorably linked.

XXVII

Our thoughts and perceptions are
what define this illusion of reality.
The very nature of self is but a mere
reference point of perception and is
fleeting and temporary.

XXVIII

Our spiritual work is to 'cleanse the
doors of perception' by reconnecting
our separate finite self to the Oneness
of the Universe and all creation.

XXIX

This potential of mystical union is activated when conscious, loving attention is wielded to create and generate the healing intention of humility and compassion in the mind and heart space.

XXX

Humility is the seed of awakening. Compassion is its fruits.

XXXI

Compassion and humility are contin-
uous reminders that this world and all
beings who live within it are here for
each other; indeed, *we are each other.*

XXXII

When the heart feels a part of all be-
ings, then the mind can finally let go
of fear. When the separate self feels
that it is a part of the divine matrix of
all creation, the ego can finally be still.

XXXIII

The profound and healing transformation of mind, from fear to love, from conflict to peace, from separation to unity, happens through polishing the mirror of your perception to see your true nature as spiritual and soul and not material.

XXXIV

When you behold this clear light of understanding, you no longer struggle with life. The shadows of this world no longer bind you. You feel the truth of Oneness in your heart and this truth sets you free.

XXXV

Every day you are on this planet you feel great bliss and joy. You shine as a beacon of truth. You radiate deep respect and gratitude. You become a bearer of forgiveness, healing, and love.

XXXVI

When the shadows of fear that separate your heart from others are dissolved, you create an enlightened paradigm of thought and reality—one illuminated in Oneness.

XXXVII

When the shadows of fear that separate yourself from your own heart are dissolved, you experience yourself as part of this infinite Oneness.

XXXVIII

May this truth of Oneness heal your heart and thereby heal our entire planet and all of humanity.

Philip M. Berk is a counsellor, a poet and writer, Reiki Master, and seeker of spiritual truth. He has always had a strong passion for spirituality. Berk's poetry inspires the human spirit to create a more meaningful and fulfilling life. Drawing from the timeless wisdom of the ages, Philip distills these teachings and presents them in a contemporary and modern voice, filled with an abundance of compassion and insight. Previously, he has written three other books entitled *Mountain Stillness, River's Wisdom: A Compassionate Guide to the Art of Being* (2008), Foreword Magazine's finalist, *Letting The Light In: Transforming Your Pain Into Power* (2010), and *The Way is Love* (2016). He currently lives in Adelaide, South Australia with his beautiful wife and two lovely daughters.

www.philipmberk.com
instagram: @philipmberk

heartwisdompress.com | heartwisdompress.com.au

heart wisdom
press

CPSIA information can be obtained
at www.ICGtesting.com
Printed in the USA
BVHW031629261020
591850BV00002B/312